BEASTS OF MYTH
AND MYSTERY

Beasts of Myth and Mystery

Michael St John Parker
Andrew Jamieson

WESSEX BOOKS

A Member of the Independent Publishers Guild

With thanks to Becky and Peter,
who had the inspiration for this book

For the illustrations in this book the publishers gratefully thank Andrew Jamieson, and for the text Michael St John Parker. Historical drawings were supplied by Mary Evans Picture Library, pp. 2, 6, 7, 9, 16, 23, 24, 39, 47 and 52.

First published in the United Kingdom in 2007 by Wessex Books

Design and layout by Wessex Books and KF:D Ltd
Computer graphics added by Alexander Grenfell on pp. 51, 55 and 57

Printed in India

ISBN 9781903035191

Contents

Beasts of Myth
and Mystery

What Is a Myth?

MANY PEOPLE THINK A MYTH IS JUST SOMETHING IMAGINED – a made-up story, or fantasy, often involving weird creatures and supernatural effects. So the adventures of the Hobbits, or Harry Potter, or even Lara Croft, are sometimes described as 'mythical'. But these are not really myths: they are fictions, stories imagined by an author who does not claim that they are true, or perhaps even realistic.

A real myth is something much more complicated than a work of fiction. It is a way of describing inherited ideas about historical happenings and about systems of ideas – real happenings, sometimes of great significance, such as the rise and fall of civilisations, and crucially important ideas such as beliefs about the forces of nature. Nobody ever 'invents' myths, in the sense that J.R.R.Tolkien or J.K.Rowling can invent the characters and the happenings in their tales; instead, real myths arise from the ways in which people talk about, or celebrate, matters that they already believe, or think they know.

Stories such as *The Lord of the Rings* can resemble myths, of course, because they draw on the language and the imagery of what might be called the real thing. Perhaps these stories satisfy the need, which everyone feels more or less, to experience the stirrings of deep fears, and excitements, and other emotions, from which we can sometimes release ourselves by hearing about imaginary situations and imaginary acts. But what might be called a living myth is regarded by those who talk about it as true, not imaginary, to the point where it may even be regarded as something rather like a cliché.

Myths do not live for ever, though. In fact, the landscape of the world's history is littered with the remains of myths that have died, either because they lost a battle for survival with a 'better' myth, or because the people who 'owned' them have themselves died out. Dead myths often linger on, however, as legends – folk-tales, ghost stories and fairy tales, quaint relics that people like to hear about but which nobody takes as literal truth.

It is the purpose of this book to describe some of the creatures which populated the myths of our ancestors, though we now see them as no more than legends. It will be important to remember that the monsters which populate these pages were not in themselves the myths: a myth is a story, and the monsters were only characters in tales which were sometimes simple, more often immensely elaborate, usually disturbing, and always very important to the people who used to tell them to each other.

The Mingling of Myths

Just as the mythical monsters in this book often combine the characteristics of different animals – horses with eagles' wings, for example – so myths themselves are often hybrids, mingling elements from different stories. This frequently came about when one tribe invaded the territory of another and conquered it; each tribe would have its own stock of stories, and over a period of time they would tend to merge with each other. For example, the first inhabitants' tales about the deeds of some superhuman figure who was credited with shaping the rivers and mountains and other features in their land might be adopted by the incoming conquerors – with the difference that the central character now became one of their own tribe.

It is sometimes possible to see the process of myth-mingling taking place, so to speak, before one's eyes. The Greek writer Herodotus, who lived in the fifth century BC, begins his account of the long rivalry between the inhabitants of the Greek islands and the neighbouring Asiatic mainland with a story about the abduction of a princess called Io; this he gives first 'according to the Persian account' – but, he goes on, 'the Greeks have a different story'. The myth had not yet consolidated into one hybrid account.

This process of mingling may even account for some of the monsters themselves – for example, when the Centaurs first appear in the Greek myths they seem not to have had the half-horse bodies by which the Romans knew them ; this may have been because of a story imported from Egypt, and added to the original legend.

How Did Monsters Matter?

When we look carefully at the ancient myths, we can see that the significance attached to monster-figures has varied considerably from time to time. In ancient Classical myths, the stories told by the Greeks and the Romans, monsters were, generally speaking, individuals – there was only one Minotaur, one Pegasus, one Hydra, one Chimaera. They often represented the forces of nature. For the people who spoke and wrote about them, therefore, they possessed superhuman powers and were capable of dominating mankind in fearful ways. Yet they were also ultimately susceptible to man's cunning and were sometimes vulnerable to human actions. The gods, who meddled continuously in human affairs, might employ monsters to give effect to their wishes; such interventions were greatly feared.

The imagination of the Nordic peoples who shaped early mediaeval Europe, after the collapse of the Roman Empire, seems to have worked in rather different ways. They feared the horrors that may lurk in watery depths – Grendel, the lake-dwelling monster whom Beowulf fought and killed, or the Midgard sea serpent whose coming will herald the end of the world – but their principal symbols of terror tended to take more human forms – trolls and ogres, dwarves and gnomes, elves and pixies. Nor was there just one of each of these – they were types, rather than individuals, which meant that any ordinary human might meet one, at any time. They were hazards of the dark forests of northern Europe, and sometimes of the lonely ocean deeps, rather than of the volcanic, earthquake-shaken shores of the Mediterranean.

With the triumph of Christianity in mediaeval Europe, monsters were cast more and more in the role of demons sent by the Devil to tempt and terrify mankind. Myths involving evil fiends, in various forms, played important parts in the minds of mediaeval men and women, as we can see from the grotesque and often terrifying shapes carved on the outsides of churches (notice, the monsters could not break into the holy house of God).

As Europeans began to explore the wider world, from the fifteenth century onwards, monsters came to be seen in yet another light: they might be no more than just those of God's creatures which were not commonly found in Europe – after all, is a griffen or a dragon so much less likely than a giraffe or a crocodile? Instead of avoiding them as evil, monsters were for a while eagerly sought by adventurers – who were quite as likely to make up stories to excite the people back at home, as to confess that that they had failed in their quests.

And with that, our monsters begin to move from the status of myth to that of legend.

A red dragon was a badge of the mediaeval Welsh princes, and after the accession of the Welsh Tudors to the English throne in 1485 the dragon took a prominent place in English royal heraldry – it made a particularly suitable supporter for the shield of Henry VIII.

CLASSICAL BEASTS

So much of modern life has been moulded by the cultures of ancient Greece and Rome that the world of classical antiquity can seem deceptively familiar. We are – or think we are – knowledgeable about Roman baths and villas, and gladiators, and dissolute emperors such as Nero; about Greek temples, and triremes, and the Trojan War, and perhaps even philosophers such as Plato. But the religious beliefs of the ancients, their myths of creation, of fate, of the forces of nature – these are less familiar territories, and when we venture into them we are often bewildered by the blood-boltered terrors we encounter.

First and foremost, of course, our awareness of classical mythology has been overlaid by centuries of Christianity, so that even where evidence of pre-Christian beliefs is available for our inspection, we may find it difficult to read or comprehend. But what is more, the culture of classical antiquity was not confined to, or even rooted in, Athens and Rome. As one modern scholar has pointed out, when Sophocles spoke of our most advanced achievements – 'language and wind-swift thought and city-dwelling habits' – he was referring to a heritage of whose antiquity he had no conception. Many civilisations had contributed to this heritage, from the fourth millennium BC onwards – in particular the Sumerians, the Hittites, the Assyrians and the Persians, and the successive generations of Egyptians.

We cannot be surprised, therefore, if the mythical monsters of the ancient world seem to our modern eyes to have a powerfully alien quality, despite the possible familiarity of their names. These are the stark, fierce relics of a pre-Christian, pre-European world; they embody the terrors, and the aspirations, that possessed the minds of man in the emergent city-civilisations of Mesopotamia and Egypt at the dawn of history.

THE HYDRA

IN THE HYDRA MYTH, THE MONSTER SEEMS TO HAVE HAD A relatively short career – which may imply that the story refers to a specific event, or episode, rather than forming part of a general picture of the natural world. However, the origins of the creature as given in the 'Theogony' (an account of the myths of the Greeks, attributed to the poet Hesiod and written around the eighth century BC) seem to imply that the Hydra was, to begin with, a symbol for an aspect of nature. There is a possibility that two different strands of myth have become inter-twined here.

The Hydra was a many-headed water-snake, the child of two other snake-monsters, Typhon and Echidne; the forms taken by this alarming family may indicate that they originally derived from an oriental creation myth rather than a Greek source. She is said to have been born under a plane-tree, and to have infested a marsh close to the source of the River Lerna, near Argos in the Greek Peloponnese.

Heracles was set the task of killing the Hydra, as his second Labour. He experienced great difficulty in subduing the monster, because every time he cut off one of its heads (the authorities disagree over the number of heads that faced him at the beginning), two more grew in its place. Eventually, Heracles' supporter Iolaus adopted the ingenious device of searing the Hydra's wounds with burning brands, which stopped them from sprouting fresh growths.

One interpretation of the myth is that it refers to an actual land (or, perhaps, marsh) clearance, aided by fire and involving the destruction of a particularly poisonous colony of snakes. A more subtle interpretation suggests that there was a fertility cult, perhaps of a sort very hostile to the uninitiated, centred on the plane-grove close to the River Lerna, and that this was suppressed with violence at some point by a tribe of invaders, who burnt down the grove and slaughtered its worshippers. The results, in any case, seem to have been long-lasting: we are told that Heracles dipped his arrows in the monster's venom, and found that every wound that they inflicted when he used them thereafter, proved fatal.

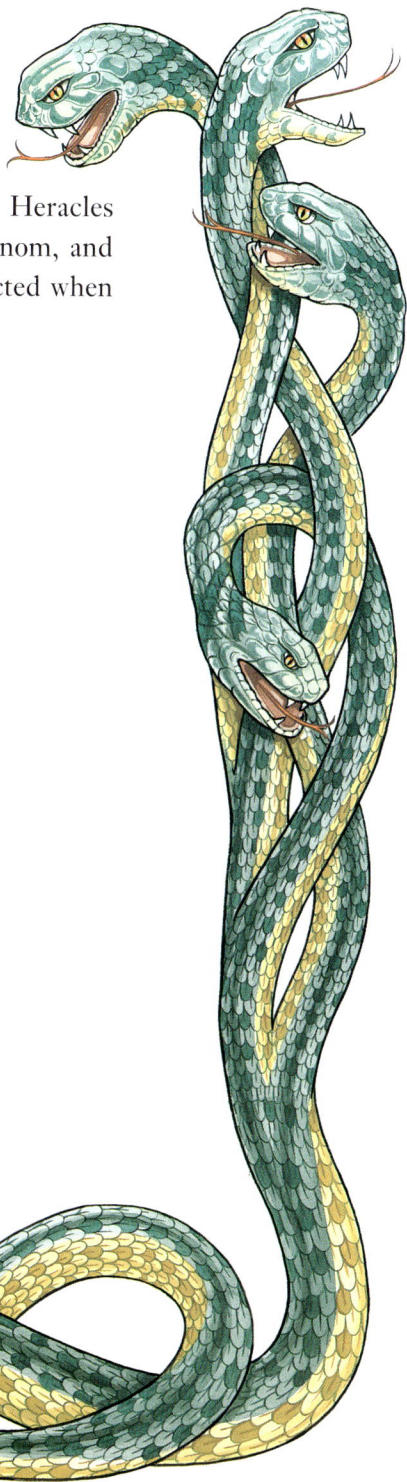

(Greek *hudōr*, 'water'.) A many-headed water snake of the Lernaen marshes in Argolia.

THE SPHINX

EVERYONE KNOWS OF THE IMAGE OF THE SPHINX WHICH BROODS enigmatically over the desert sands in Egypt. And everyone, almost, has heard of the riddle of the Sphinx – even if they are not quite sure what the question was, or what the answer. But the Sphinx posed her riddle at Thebes, in Greece, not in Egypt. So what is her image doing beside the pyramids?

Part of the answer is that the cult of the Sphinx was widespread for many centuries all over the ancient Near East. She was a death-dealing deity (her name means 'the Strangler') who was feared throughout the civilisations of the Nile, Tigris and Euphrates river valleys. In the form of a lion with a woman's head and bust, and the wings of an eagle, she is found guarding gates, and decorating the bits and harness-rings of horses, in Mesopotamia as well as Egypt, from at least 2000 BC.

The Sphinx appears in Greek mythology as the result of a union between two other primitive deities, Typhon ('stupefying smoke', a volcano-god) and Echidne (a serpent-woman). Or her parents may have been Orthrus (the Dog-star) and Echidne – or Orthrus and Chimaera; the genealogy is confused to say the least, but it has been suggested that in this stage of the myth the Sphinx has become a calendar-symbol, recording a momentous decision on the part of a priestly caste to organise a sacred year in two phases, indicated by the two elements of the Sphinx's body.

The human element enters the Sphinx myth with the tragic hero Oedipus, who released the city of Thebes from the tyranny of the Sphinx by solving her riddle, whereupon the Sphinx hurled herself in fury from the high rock on which she perched, and so dashed herself to death. Oedipus, for his part, was acclaimed as king by the Thebans, and married the queen whom he had recently widowed – not knowing that the king he had killed was his own father, and the queen, his mother.

The Sphinx of Greek mythology was a monster with the head and breasts of a woman, the body of a dog or lion, the wings of a bird, a serpent's tail and lion's paws.

The Egyptian sphinx was a lion with a pharoah's head.

THE RIDDLE OF THE SPHINX:
What goes on four feet, on two feet, and three,
But the more feet it goes on the weaker it be?

Human stages from infancy to old age.

THE HARPY

*Of monsters all, most monstrous this; no greater wrath
God sends 'mongst men;
it comes from depth of pitchy Hell;
And virgin's face, but wombe like gulf unsatiate hath,
Her hands are griping claws, her colour pale and fell.*

S O RUNS A SEVENTEENTH-CENTURY TRANSLATION OF A PASSAGE IN the Roman poet Virgil, describing the dreaded Harpy. The name itself comes from a Greek word meaning 'snatcher', and for early writers such as Homer the Harpies seem to have been violent winds, bearing names such as Ocypete (the swift flyer) and Aello (the storm wind), who were the children of sea-gods. They were shown in sculptures as birds with the faces of women – and this was a form often given, also, to the souls of the dead, who were believed to snatch away the breath of the living.

The hero Jason, with his Argonauts, in the course of his quest for the Golden Fleece, is said to have driven away two Harpies who were persecuting a blind Thracian king, Phineus, by stealing the food from his tables. Here the myth seems to have incorporated a description of the Thracians' habit of putting out food for the sea-eagles whom they regarded as sacred – and a story about a wife who was trying to starve her husband to death.

Like other monsters of the ancient classical world, the Harpy came to feature in the fantastic world of mediaeval heraldry – though it cannot have been a badge of which the bearer would have been particularly proud. An early writer on heraldic matters opined that 'The Harpy should be given to such persons as have committed manslaughter, to the end that by the often view of their Ensigns they might be moved to bewail the foulness of their offence'.

These days Harpies are predatory women – or, for the eighteenth-century lexicographer Dr Johnson, the agents of government taxation.

THE HARPY

THE MINOTAUR

THE MYTH OF THE MINOTAUR IS, HISTORICALLY, ABOUT THE tense relationship between the rulers of Crete at the beginning of the second millennium BC and the inhabitants of the colony which the Cretans had established at Athens.

The Cretan kings, whose name (or, perhaps, title) was Minos, required the Athenians to supply an annual tribute of young people (probably a group of hostages). The Athenians struggled against this demand, and their representative hero, Theseus, eventually defeated the Cretans, partly by bravery and partly by guile, and married the daughter of Minos – who, since this was a matrilineal society, brought with her the inheritance of the kingdom.

At another level, the story depicts the playing out of a complex religious ritual concerned with the annual renewal of fertility and the transfer of authority from one generation to another. The Athenian version of the story presents the Cretan tyranny in symbolic form as a Minotaur, a man with a bull's head. The Cretan kings masqueraded as bulls in an annual fertility ritual during which they coupled with a cow-priestess. The Minotaur is said to have inhabited a labyrinth, or maze, which may have represented, for its Athenian attackers, the complexity of the huge royal palace at Knossos, in Crete; however, maze-dances featured in many ancient religious rituals, and have left their mark all over Europe (they were still taking place, in simplified forms drained of any meaning, among schoolchildren in Britain in the nineteenth century. On St Catherine's Hill near Winchester the turf maze can still be seen). The Athenian hero destroys the Minotaur with the help of Minos' daughter, Ariadne; her name signifies 'the very holy one', and suggests that she is in fact the moon-priestess with whom the successor-king had to couple before he could succeed to the throne.

The Cretans, we are told, denied that there ever was such a monster as the Minotaur. But then they would, wouldn't they?

(Greek *Minōtaurus*, 'bull of Minos'.) A mythical monster with the head of a bull and the body of a man.

PEGASUS

THE MYTH OF PEGASUS, THE WINGED HORSE, IS A PARTICULARLY good demonstration of the way in which real history can be preserved and handed down by way of stories about heroes and supernatural creatures.

Early in the second millennium BC, the area that we now know as Greece was invaded by a race of people called Hellenes. They were organised along patriarchal lines; their rulers were men and their family structures gave primacy to men over women. But the society which they conquered was a matriarchy, ruled by queens who were priestesses of the moon-goddess; the priestesses wore terrifying masks to repel strangers; the horse, with its moon-shaped hooves, was an animal revered by the moon cult. The Hellenes killed the priestesses and took over the sacred horses for their own purposes.

In the mythical account of this historical process, Perseus (a Hellene, whose name meant 'the Destroyer') killed the Gorgon Medusa (a masked priestess, or a manifestation of the moon-goddess). From Medusa's blood sprang the winged horse, Pegasus (fresh power for the conquering Hellenes); he was the fruit of a union between Medusa and the sea-god, Poseidon (the Hellenes were great sea-farers).

Pegasus subsequently bore another hero, Bellerophon, to defeat the Chimaera. But Bellerophon eventually became over-bold, and presumed to invade Olympus itself, the home of the gods. Zeus therefore sent a gadfly (a small but vicious insect, and a symbol of Zeus' contempt) to sting Pegasus, who reared and threw Bellerophon back to earth. Zeus took over the winged horse for his own use, and now employs him to carry his thunderbolts.

The winged horse of Greek legend. In the Second World War the horse with Bellerophon on his back, in pale blue on a maroon background, was adopted as the insignia of all British airborne troops.

THE CHIMAERA

THE CHIMAERA HAD THREE HEADS, FROM EACH OF WHICH IT breathed fire; the foremost head was that of a lion, and it had a lion's legs; the second head, and the main part of its body, was that of a goat; and its tail, which ended in the third head, was that of a serpent. It inhabited a region to the north of Greece called Lycia, where it blasted the countryside and all the inhabitants with its fiery breath.

Eventually a hero, named Bellerophon, who came from Greece, promised the king of Lycia that he would destroy this monster. With the aid of the goddess Athene, Bellerophon bridled the winged horse Pegasus, who carried him high into the air above the Chimaera so that he was able to shoot the monster with arrows from his bow before thrusting between her jaws a lump of lead, which melted in her fiery breath and trickled into her vitals, destroying her.

This complicated myth has been explained in various ways. An

eighteenth-century scholar, John Lempriere, suggested that it should be explained by 'the recollection that there was a burning mountain [volcano], in Lycia, whose top was the resort of lions, on account of its desolate wilderness; the middle, which was fruitful, was covered with goats; and at the bottom the marshy ground abounded with serpents. Bellerophon is said to have conquered the Chimaera, because he cultivated the mountain.'

On a more modern interpretation, the three heads of the monster are symbols from an ancient calendar by which the year was divided into three parts. The oldest depiction of the Chimaera, on a glass plaque found near Mycenae in Crete, comes from a period when kings were required to fight for their thrones each year, as part of a fertility ritual. This might suggest that Bellerophon's victory symbolises the triumph of a new, vigorous hero over the natural forces of the seasons.

(Greek *khimaira*, 'she-goat'). A fabulous monster in Greek mythology. It has a lion's head, a goat's body and a dragon's tail (Homer).

THE CENTAUR

Of all the monsters of antiquity, the centaurs had, perhaps, the most mixed reputation. They were often credited with great wisdom and prophetic skill, and their leader, Cheiron, was revered as a teacher whose pupils included Achilles, the mighty warrior, Jason, the hero of the adventure of the Golden Fleece, and Aesculapius, the wonder-working physician. On the other hand, the Centaurs seem to have been wild, turbulent and dangerous, and they were the cause of two famous episodes of battle, namely the struggle with the Lapiths (when drunken Centaurs inexcusably disrupted a wedding feast), and their fight with Heracles (when the Centaurs attacked Heracles against the laws of hospitality).

The Centaurs combined the body of a horse with the torso and head of a man – though many representations show their lower parts as more goatish than horse-like. This description, taken with their strange mingling of wisdom with disorderly behaviour, suggests that they may have been enduring versions of the anarchic animal figures which danced in mock opposition to a newly-installed king in early Hellenic rituals. Of course, the myth may also embody memories of actual historic episodes of conflict between the Hellenes and the neolithic mountain tribes whom they displaced.

But there may be a still older element in the myth of the Centaurs. The horse was sacred to the moon, the moon was believed to control the rain, and so many ancient people have performed horse dances to make rain fall when it was needed. Should we see our springtime hobby-horses as the last survivors of the Centaurs?

Centaurs are said to have dwelt in ancient Thessaly, where there were many expert horsemen. The Thessalian centaurs were invited to a marriage feast: one of them tried to abduct the bride, conflict ensued, and the centaurs were driven out of the country.

NORDIC BEASTS

IF THE CIVILISATIONS THAT DEVELOPED IN ANCIENT EGYPT AND Mesopotamia were expressive of life in the teeming cities of the great river-plains, our North European culture can, by contrast, be seen almost as an affair of individuals dwelling in a wilder but more hospitable landscape, men and women strongly disposed to independence if often lacking in sophistication. This emphasis on the value of the individual was hugely reinforced – perhaps, indeed, it was actually created – by the influence of Christian thought and practice.

The difference is apparent as soon as we look at the mythical creatures of the North. Many of them are simply manifestations of the worst traits of men themselves, and resemble men in their forms – for example, cruelty (ogres), stupidity (giants), lust (mermaids), cunning (dwarves) or avarice (gnomes). Nobler elements in the human character are also given shape – helpfulness (pixies), gentleness (fairies – some of them, at least), bravery (elves). Seen in this light, the development of the Christian belief in angels provides an interesting example of North European myth-making in action: the pre-Christian 'ancestors' of angels, as found among the civilisations of the ancient Near East, were often rather threatening, even malevolent spirits, but Christian theologians progressively turned them into pure emanations of divine virtue and goodwill.

There were other myths, too, concerning the dangers which lurked in the wild places inhabited by the hardy individualists of the North. Hunters, mountaineers and sailors all knew that there were dreadful creatures to be found in the forest, the mountain and the sea. But these were perceived as material beings, fearfully dangerous but ultimately vulnerable to the sword of a brave man – whereas the monsters of the ancient world were the irresistible forces of nature itself.

ELVES

THE MYTHOLOGY OF NORTHERN EUROPE CAN SEEM SIMPLER and more coherent than that of the Mediterranean civilisations, if only because there are fewer strands running through it. But there is still scope for confusion. For example, the Elves are found to be of two sorts, one of which, the Black, or Night, Elves is in fact the race of Dwarves.

But there are White Elves also, and these are described in the Eddas, or collections of mythological tales which were compiled in Scandinavia between 1056 and 1640, as the White Elves, or Elves of Light. They lived in Alfheim, the kingdom of the sun-god Freyr. In appearance they were exceedingly fair, and shone with a dazzling brilliance; they usually resembled lovely children, clad in delicate, transparent garments. They were kindly disposed to mankind.

It is not always easy to distinguish between Elves and Fairies, except by suggesting that Elves are more significant, powerful, and important in human affairs than the little, fluttering Fairies. The English poet Edmund Spenser, who wrote in the later sixteenth century, gave Elves an heroic role when he described them as the knights of his imagined 'faery land', and these, clearly, were also the Elves that J.R.R. Tolkien had in mind when he wrote *The Lord of the Rings*.

Elves were credited with many of the little inexplicable wonders of the world; for example, the fossils called belemnites, and the flint arrow-heads left behind by Stone Age man, were both thought to have been made by Elves, and were called elf-bolts or elf-arrows.

Originally dwarfish beings of Germanic mythology, elves were possessed of magical powers which they used for the good or ill of mankind.

DWARVES AND GNOMES

IT MAY SEEM UNFAIR TO CLASSIFY DWARVES AS MONSTERS, WHEN they are, actually, very small; but the word 'monsters' really signifies something marvellous or extraordinary, rather than just huge. It would be still more unfair if the Dwarves in this book were to be confused with the very small people who may be seen in our streets any day of the week; for present purposes, Dwarves are definitely supernatural beings. Of course, it must be true that the legends about Dwarves were prompted, to a considerable extent, by the desire to explain why there are such small people in the first case.

Dwarves are figures in Scandinavian mythology (the myths of the Mediterranean region do not seem to feature any really equivalent creatures). We are told that there was a primeval giant, at the beginning of time, called Ymir, who was the father of a race of frost-giants; but when he died, there emerged from his body (like the maggots that crawl from a decaying corpse) a race of tiny people, who dwelt underground in caverns and hollow hills. These Dwarves were the first technologists – they were skilled with tools, and could work metal, as well as digging mines; perhaps significantly in this context, they were partly good and partly evil.

Gnomes are much the same as Dwarves; they, too, inhabit the subterranean regions, where they guard the treasures of the earth, particularly its gold. (Hence our mischievous nickname for today's Swiss bankers – the Gnomes of Zurich!)

A variant type of 'overground Dwarf' appears in English literature from the late sixteenth century onwards, most famously under the name of Tom Thumb. He is a lively, mischievous, essentially good-natured, at times even heroic, miniature person, who survives extraordinary adventures with the help of a fairy godmother and the gift of making himself invisible. He is the central figure of innumerable folk stories – apparently his name has been more frequently employed than that of any other character in nursery literature – and he often ends up in triumph, marrying a beautiful princess or inheriting a hoard of golden treasure. He is the original little man who wins the lottery!

Dwarves were guardians of mineral wealth and precious stones and very skilful at their work. They are prominent in Germanic and Scandinavian legend and generally dwelt in rocks and caves and recesses of the earth.

GIANTS, TROLLS AND OGRES

THE OVERSIZED AND THE UNDERSIZED ALWAYS FASCINATE, AND sometimes frighten us, so it is hardly surprising that the myths of antiquity were rich in huge super-humans. The Titans appear very early, in Babylonian astrology, where they are identified with the planets; they may have been introduced to Greece by a colony of Hittites who settled the Isthmus of Corinth early in the second millennium BC; they were certainly worshipped for a time in that region. The Giants, strictly speaking, were a different group, earth-born monsters who assailed the gods on Olympus and who were destroyed by Heracles.

There does not seem to be a direct mythological link between the Giant figures of Mediterranean antiquity and those of northern Europe, where their legends are widespread and very varied. The northern Giants are occasionally genial, but mostly ferocious, cruel – and stupid; they are reassuringly vulnerable to the bravery of an ingenious man.

Scandinavian mythology features Trolls, huge creatures of peculiar malice and cruelty who dwelt in the hills. (In Denmark and Sweden, however, the type underwent a remarkable transformation, shrinking in size to become imps, who lived in caves or holes in the ground.)

Ogres are French man-eating monsters. The name is of ancient origin, but its first recorded appearance in print is in the *Histoires ou Contes du Temps Passé* of Charles Perrault, in 1697. Perrault was a leading light in a remarkable movement to popularise folk-tales and legends of many sorts, which provides a fascinating counterpart to the rise of scientific thought and rational philosophy. In England, the tales of Jack the Giant-Killer, and Jack and the Bean Stalk, seem to have been first collected, organised, adorned and expanded for publication around 1708.

Giants are people well above normal height and size. The belief that mankind has degenerated – 'There were giants in the earth in those days' (Genesis 6:4) – was ingrained among primitive peoples.

Troll (Old Norse *troll*, 'demon'.) In Icelandic myth a troll was a malignant, sometimes one-eyed, giant with a propensity for stealing.

Ogres. Giants of very malignant disposition, who live on human flesh.

GRENDEL

THE POEM CALLED 'BEOWULF' IS TO ANGLO-SAXON CIVILISATION what 'The Iliad' is to the Greeks. Written during the eighth century AD, it concerns the doings of kings and their warriors in Denmark and Sweden – several of them are historic characters who are known to have lived in the sixth century, and we can identify the site of the great royal hall, Heorot, where much of the early action of the poem takes place.

This Nordic tale resembles classical myths of the Mediterranean region in that it embodies traditions about historical events. But 'Beowulf' is a myth built around specifically Christian ideas; it is one of the most significant achievements of early European literature.

Grendel, the monster who is at the centre of the action in the opening phase of the poem, is half-man, half-fiend;

a notorious ranger of the borderlands, who inhabited the fastnesses of moors and fens. This unhappy being had long lived in the land of monsters, because God had damned him along with the children of Cain. For the eternal Lord avenged the killing of Abel. He took no delight in that feud, but banished Cain from humanity because of his crime. From Cain were hatched all evil progenies: ogres, hobgoblins and monsters, not to mention the giants who fought so long against God – for which they suffered due retribution.

The hero Beowulf grapples with Grendel when the monster raids Heorot, and wounds him mortally. This proves, however, to be only the beginning of a sequence of trials and struggles; Grendel's mother takes up the battle, and, later in the poem, Beowulf has to confront a terrible, fire-breathing, gold-guarding dragon.

All these monsters are representations of the evil against which man must ever be prepared to do battle. The structure and meaning of this great epic have been brilliantly analysed by J.R.R. Tolkien, the author of *The Lord of the Rings*, who drew on 'Beowulf' for much of his own inspiration.

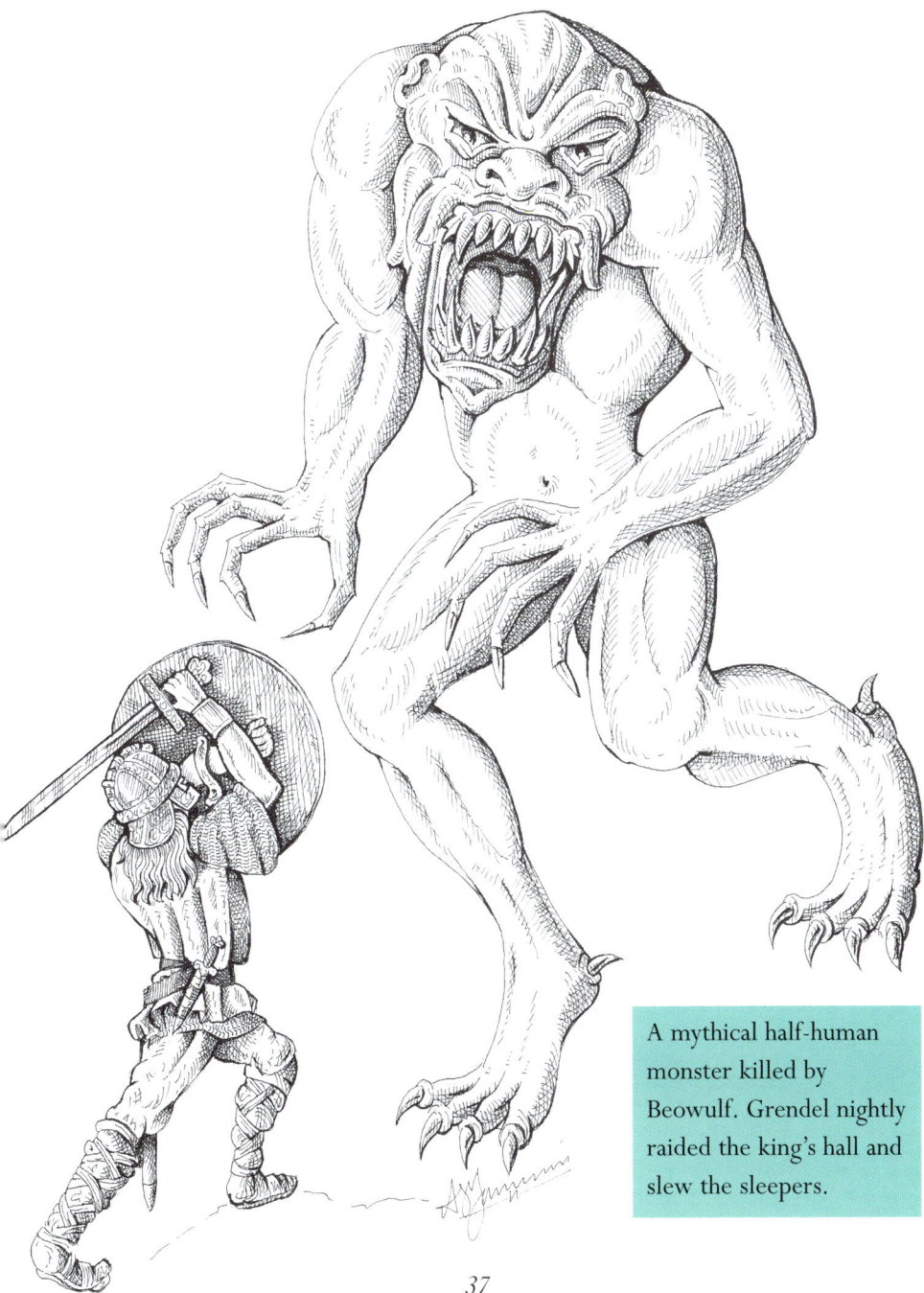

A mythical half-human monster killed by Beowulf. Grendel nightly raided the king's hall and slew the sleepers.

THE MERMAID

THE LIFE OF A SEA-FARER IN THE DAYS OF SAIL WAS USUALLY hard and often dangerous; but worse than all the perils of the sea, according to the sailors themselves, was the lack of female company on long voyages. So who can blame them for imagining their hearts' desire?

> *Our anchor was new weighed,*
> *And our ship not far from the land,*
> *When I espied a fair pretty maid,*
> *With a comb and a glass in her hand.*

And how bewitchingly she sang! All agreed that the song of the Mermaid was wonderfully sweet – and she seemed to sing particularly for men who had left wives behind at home. But woe betide the mariner who allowed himself to be lured by this song, or by the beauties of the Mermaid's upper half; being 'married to a Mermaid' meant drowning. Here was a myth with a moral, if ever there was one!

Stories of Mermaids have a long history among the seagoing populations of western Europe. In their earliest versions, they seem to relate Mermaids to the Sirens who had tried to draw the Greek hero Odysseus out of his ship to his death; but whereas the Sirens were half-birds, Mermaids were half-fish and lived in the depths of the sea rather than on an island.

Mermaids appear in mediaeval church carvings, in illuminated manuscripts, and even on coats of arms – always with comb and looking-glass in hand, to indicate their vain and tricky temperaments.

Suggestions that the myth of the Mermaid may be derived from sightings of the dugong, or manatee, a real sea-creature with a faint resemblance to a fish-woman, can be dismissed as boringly unromantic.

A Jaimieson

THE SEA SERPENT

BY COMPARISON WITH THE MYTHICAL MONSTERS OF ANCIENT Greece and Rome, the Sea Serpent is really quite a simple creature. It does not enshrine facts about complicated historical events, or symbolise subtle beliefs about the calendar or the seasons. It simply reminds us of the fearful mysteries that lurk in the unfathomable oceans, and of the desperate perils that faced the deep-sea mariner in the days of sail.

From earliest times, sea-farers have been disposed to believe in sea-monsters, and with good reason. The reality of marine life is startling enough: huge whales, monstrous squids, sharks of appalling ferocity, and, sometimes surfacing after submarine upheavals, denizens of the deep so weird and frightening in their appearance that it would not take an unduly imaginative mind to see them as the creations of the Devil.

To an ignorant, superstitious, apprehensive sailor who was, perhaps unwillingly, embarked on a voyage of exploration, very conscious of the frailty of his little wooden vessel and of the immensity of the ocean ('No bottom, no bottom with this line!'), and very much aware of the alarming stories to be found in no less an authority than the Holy Bible, the great Sea Serpent must have seemed more of a probability than a possibility.

And if the sailor's own fears were not enough to make him imagine impending disaster, there were plentiful accounts circulating during the centuries of exploration, between *c*1450 and *c*1850, many of them claiming support from near-eye-witnesses, of boats, and even full-sized ships, that had been suddenly attacked, overwhelmed by dreadful, snaky coils, and dragged down to their doom.

Indeed, there are those who still keep a corner of their mind open on this subject. After all, if the sea can astound science with a coelacanth, why not a Sea Serpent . . .?

The Sea Serpent is a serpentine monster said to inhabit the depth of the ocean. It is sometimes thought of as a Leviathan.

THE GREEN MAN

THE EYES THAT LOOK OUT OF THE MASK OF LEAVES ARE sometimes disconcertingly bold, sometimes disagreeably furtive, sometimes chillingly indifferent and aged: what does the Green Man mean? No-one knows – this is one of the most enigmatic of myths, but also one of the most persistent in northern Europe.

The first literary reference in English to the Green Man comes in 1638, but his carved or painted heads, and sometimes whole figures of wild, shaggy men of the woods, are scattered throughout the iconography of mediaeval Europe. And unlike many of the devil-monsters whose effigies menace and grimace around the outsides of mediaeval churches, the Green Man was allowed inside – or perhaps he just slipped in regardless. Anyway, there he is, peering out of a boss at the intersection of a vault, or leering from the underside of the misericord on which the priest leans while chanting his psalms, or mocking the pretensions of the good and great from the corner of a tomb canopy.

As Jack-in-the-Green, he appears in mummings and folk-dancings that persist to this day – an anarchic, jovial, but also potentially disturbing figure, and one who offers a sly but explicit threat towards the girls.

The Green Man may well embody some survival of ancient nature worship – a forest deity, clothed in springtime foliage. There are strong suggestions of a fertility cult in the antics of Jack and his pursuit of the girls. But equally there are suggestions of lawless figures on the fringes of society, sidling in to play seditious roles at a public occasion – camouflaged poachers who prowl the royal forests, Robin Hood and his band of outlaws in their Lincoln green tunics.

The Green Man is the patron of subversives and survivors. He is not at all quaint, and should not be taken lightly.

The Green Man is often found in the foliated stonework and ornamented carving of medieval churches throughout Europe. It is believed to be a Celtic symbol of creative fertility in nature.

HERALDIC BEASTS

THE BEASTS OF HERALDRY ARE, IN TRUTH, RATHER A MIXED bunch; while many of them are creatures from ancient mythology, or at least can trace their ancestry to stories retailed by writers such as Herodotus, others may be seen as representing little more than the desire of mediaeval heralds to find appropriate symbols for the ferocity, or splendour, or merely the pride and ambition of the knights whose shields they blazoned.

As the disciplines of heraldry developed during the Middle Ages, monsters came to be depicted with increasing formality. In fact, many of the forms which are now customary for such well-known creatures as unicorns, dragons and griffins were shaped by mediaeval heralds, and might be found to bear slight resemblance to classical or pre-classical models.

If the appearances of the beasts have been stylised, however, to the point where the very word 'heraldic' has become synonymous with decorative artificiality, their identities may be seen as having undergone subtle reinforcement, partly by way of transference. As many modern logo-owning bodies have found, often to their delight and sometimes to their alarm, identity can be affected, as well as expressed, by images. Ask a Welsh rugby player what a dragon means to him!

Where they appear in coats of arms, monsters are depicted in order to draw attention to some characteristic of the bearer of the shield, or of his family's history; they do not appear for their own sake. By the same token, they may be shown in various postures, each of which carries its own significance; parts of them, only, may be displayed – a head wrenched from its body, or a torso chopped in half; colourings, too, may be varied according to the laws of heraldry, to carry different shades of meaning. With the development of heraldry, therefore, the monster becomes an artistic creation, rather than an object of true fear; so he passes from myth into legend.

THE DRAGON

(Greek *drakön*) is related to *drakos*, 'eye').
A dragon is a fabulous winged crocodile often with a serpent's tail. In medieval romance captive ladies were often guarded by dragons.

MYTHS INVOLVING DRAGONS ARE VERY WIDESPREAD. HARDLY anywhere in the world, from Persia to Peru, or from Beijing in China to Burley Beacon in Hampshire, seems to be without its legend of fearful, scaly, serpentine monsters with leathery wings, four taloned feet, and a long, lashing tail. (The Dragons of Christian art breathe fire, as well – but not all the time.)

Many ingenious theories have been put forward to explain why Dragons are so 'common'. There are, of course, various creatures of the lizard family which might be said to resemble Dragons – and, though they are found only in certain tropical regions, it has been suggested that the Dragon myth perpetuates folk-memories of their much greater and more widely-distributed ancestors.

More likely, perhaps, is the identification of Dragons with meteorites or lightning strikes ; indeed, the same word was used for all three in fifteenth-century Wales. In 735 AD, the Annals of Ulster recorded that 'A huge dragon was seen, with great thunder after it, at the end of autumn'; surely this was a meteorological monster.

The Dragons of Europe, in particular, were closely associated with volcanic eruptions – hence their fire-breathing characteristic. But their tendency to hoard treasures of gold may have been borrowed from the Griffins.

On one thing almost everyone was agreed: Dragons were terrible. And they posed a particular threat to beautiful maidens. The legend of St George (a figure almost as mythical as the Dragon itself) was vigorously promoted by the mediaeval Christian Church as an encouragement to the warrior class to be heroic in defence of virtue – a brilliant example of the profitable adaptation of a myth to a new purpose.

THE UNICORN

(Latin *unus* 'one', and *cornu*, 'horn'.) A mythical and heraldic animal with the legs of a buck, the tail of a lion, the head and body of a horse, and a single horn.

The unicorn has but one horn in the middle of its forehead. It is the only animal that ventures to attack the elephant; and so sharp is the nail of its foot, that with one blow it can rip the belly of the beast. Hunters can catch the unicorn only by placing a young virgin in his haunts. No sooner does he see the damsel, than he runs towards her, and lies down at her feet, and so suffers himself to be captured by the hunters.

Le Bestaire Divin de Guillaume, Clerc de Normandie (13th century)

I T HARDLY SEEMS RIGHT TO LIST THE UNICORN AS A MONSTER, FOR the myth of this beautiful beast almost always represents it as a symbol of virtue and bravery, and often also of healing.

It is usually shown as a pure white horse, with a single long horn growing from the centre of its forehead. It was said to be very shy, but gallant in conflict with evil monsters; it would submit only to a virgin girl. The touch of its horn was reputed to cure the most grievous of wounds, and fraudulent quack-doctors used to peddle the powder of what they claimed were ground-up unicorn horns as an antidote to poison.

Literal-minded people have suggested that the legend of the Unicorn arose from sightings of the oryx, a north African antelope which has two long horns that can look like one if seen in profile. Still less excitingly, the rhinoceros has been proposed as a model – after all, it is a four-legged creature which, undeniably, has a horn growing from the front of its head. The rhinoceros fails to meet the other requirements of the legend; interestingly, however, its horn, too, is credited with possessing magical qualities, and the beast has been ruthlessly hunted for it as a result. Equally prized are the tusks of the narwhal, a sea-creature which grows a single long, straight but spirally-grooved tooth which, found on its own, looks exactly like the imagined horn of the Unicorn.

The Unicorn became associated with the heraldic bearings of the Kings of Scotland from the fifteenth century onwards, and since the union of the Crowns of England and Scotland in 1603 it has appeared as one of the two 'supporters' of the royal coat of arms. As such, it appears on the 'sinister', or junior side of the shield when displayed in England, but on the 'dexter' or senior side in Scotland.

THE WYVERN

THE WYVERN IS REALLY A VARIANT OF THE DRAGON, AND ONE may suspect that it is really the creation of a herald's fevered imagination, rather than the expression of any ancient myth. Be that as it may, Wyverns are to be found gaping menacingly among the carved ornaments of many mediaeval buildings, writhing themselves around the titlepages of early printed books, and flying furiously towards nowhere in particular on the corners of the first, somewhat speculative, maps.

The Wyvern has the head of a Dragon, and its forked tongue, scaly neck and leathery wings, but it combines with these the two clawed feet of an eagle (whereas the Dragon has four), and a long, serpentine tail which is often depicted as knotted, or twined upon itself, to indicate the extreme venomousness and violent temper of the monster.

In fact the tails of both these dreadful creatures were objects of particular horror. They were thought to pollute the earth over which they trailed, so that the grass was marked and fungus grew (hence 'fairy rings'), and left loathsome slime (such as frogspawn) or distorted creatures (such as flounders) in their wake.

The Wyvern shares the Dragon's passion for treasure, and its capacity for vigilance. Like the Dragon, also, the Wyvern is said to be preternaturally hot – hence, according to a seventeenth-century authority on heraldry, who in turn took his cue from the Prophet Jeremiah (xiv, 6), the fact that Wyverns and Dragons are always shown with their mouths wide open, as if gulping the cooling air.

Today the Wyvern is used as a logo for the Wessex Society, which promotes the culture and customs of Wessex, whose boundaries are not well defined but broadly encompass Wiltshire, Dorset, Somerset and part of Hampshire.

THE GRIFFIN

THE GRIFFIN – OR GRIFFEN, OR GRIFFON, OR GRYPHON – IS A particularly ancient monster, whose images, shaped in the sixth century BC, can be found guarding the treasure-houses or sealing the records of the Achaemenian rulers of the Babylonian empire (modern Iraq and Iran). Interestingly, the Greek historian Herodotus, writing in the middle of the fifth century BC, suggests that Griffins were native to a region far to the north of the Black Sea, where they gathered and hoarded gold from the rivers; this gold was then often stolen (by a race of one-eyed men, so ran the story; but Herodotus allowed himself a commendable bout of cautiousness at this point, remarking 'I hesitate to believe in one-eyed men who in other respects are like the rest of us'), and so eventually got into circulation in the civilised world.

Wherever they originated, Griffins were guardians, whether of treasure, or of learning (the helmet of Minerva, goddess of wisdom, was often shown ornamented with a Griffin's head), or of the secrets of state. They were peculiarly fitted for this role by their combination of a lion's body with an eagle's wings, head and foreclaws – a fearsome ensemble.

Myths involving Griffins 'migrated' with little variation from one culture to another in the ancient world, and the identity of this magnificent monster was sufficiently well established for it to find a further life in the Christian period as a symbol of security and strength. It features accordingly in many coats of arms, and can still be seen performing its ancient function in almost every High Street in England, where it guards the doorways of Barclays Bank.

(From Old French *grifon*, Latin *gryphus*, Greek *grups*.) A mythical monster fabled to be the offspring of the lion and the eagle, was sacred to the sun and kept guard over hidden treasures.

THE YALE

HE HISTORY OF THE HERALDIC BEAST CALLED THE YALE IS nearly as odd as the creature itself. It is mentioned by the Roman writer Pliny, but remained obscure for many centuries thereafter, until Pliny's description sparked the imaginations of heralds who introduced it to several coats of arms in the fifteenth and sixteenth centuries in England. Then it was forgotten again, and did not appear in even the most authoritative books about heraldry, until it was 'rediscovered' in 1911.

The name given to this monster was originally 'Eale', and it should probably be pronounced as if it was spelt 'Yarlee'. Pliny's account of it runs as follows:

> The Yale is the size of a hippopotamus, with the tail of an elephant, is black or dark brown in colour, and has the jaws of a boar. It has mobile horns, more than a cubit in length, which in battle it alternately holds firm and moves, so that they are either dangerous or turned aside, as may be required.

The heralds made the Yale resemble a ferocious goat, rather than a hippopotamus, gave it a lion's tail, and developed its boar's tusks to an alarming degree.

A Yale appears as one of the supporters of the shield bearing the arms of John, Duke of Bedford, third son of King Henry IV. One of his titles, and with it the Yale, passed to the Beaufort family, and through the great heiress, Lady Margaret Beaufort, to her son, Henry VII. So the Yale is ranked as one the Royal Beasts, and appears on St George's Chapel at Windsor, and at Hampton Court. Because of the Lady Margaret, who founded St John's College, and was a benefactor of Christ's College, both in Cambridge, it also supports those colleges' coats of arms, and struts fiercely above their gates.

Yale (or water buffalo) is shown on the 12th-century Hereford Mappa Mundi in the area marked EGYPT.

THE COCKATRICE

ANYONE WHO HAS BEEN TO A CHRISTMAS CAROL SERVICE MUST have heard the prophecy of Isaiah concerning the coming of the blessed day when 'the weaned child shall put his hand on the Cockatrice' den' and suffer no hurt. This, and the other promises that accompany it, make marvellous poetry; but what is a Cockatrice? Modern translations of the Bible turn it into something like an adder – but that might not have satisfied Isaiah, or the mediaeval heralds who delighted in displaying the Cockatrice on coats of arms.

The creature has the head, neck and legs of a cockerel, fiercely beaked and crested, with a dragon's barbed tail and wings. Thus it combines angry pride with bitter venom. But it has one other, most lethal characteristic, which Shakespeare puts into Juliet's mind in Act III, Scene 2 of *Romeo and Juliet*: 'the death-darting eye of cockatrice' was the threat that Isaiah's weaned child should most fear, its ability to kill with a look.

The Roman writer Pliny asserted that the Cockatrice 'kills the shrubs, not only by contact, but by breathing on them, and splits the rocks, such power of evil is there in him'. John Guillim, a seventeenth-century writer on heraldry, went even further: 'The Cockatrice is called in Latin Regulus, for that he seemeth to be a little King amongst Serpents, not in regard of his quantity [that is, his size], but in respect of the infection of his pestiferous and poisonful aspect [that is, his glance], wherewith he poisoneth the air.'

One cannot help wondering, after all that, who would willingly bear a Cockatrice on his coat of arms. But it is a comfort to know that the Cockatrice could be defeated by a weasel – particularly if the weasel took the precaution of eating some rue before engaging in combat. It is said that Wherwell, in Hampshire, was at one time terrorised by a cockatrice, until an ingenious man held a mirror before it, and so got it to kill itself.

Cockatrice (Latin *cockatrix*). A fabulous and heraldic monster with the wings of a fowl, the tail of a dragon and the head of a cock. Otherwise known as a Basilisk.

THE PHOENIX

THE PHOENIX SEEMS TO HAVE OCCUPIED A SIGNIFICANT PLACE IN the mythology of ancient Egypt and Arabia, where it symbolised the renewal of life in long cycles. Greek philosophy paid less attention, on the whole, to this concept of cyclical renewal, and the Phoenix does not figure prominently in the Greek myths – although the name by which we know it is a Greek word, which describes its blood-red plumage.

The Romans, and in particular the mythologizing poet Ovid, showed more interest in the Phoenix. Here is what Ovid wrote:

Most beings spring from other individuals; but there is a certain kind which reproduces itself. The Assyrians call it the Phoenix. It does not live on fruit or flowers, but on frankincense and odoriferous gums. When it has lived five hundred years, it builds itself a nest in the branches of an oak, or on the top of a palm tree. In this it collects cinnamon, and spikenard, and myrrh, and of these materials builds a pile in which it deposits itself, and dying, breathes out its last breath amidst odours. From the body of the parent bird, a

young Phoenix issues forth, destined to live as long a life as its predecessor. When this has grown up and gained sufficient strength, it lifts its nest from the tree (its own cradle and its parent's sepulchre), and carries it to the city of Heliopolis in Egypt, and deposits it in the temple of the Sun.

Ovid's account helped to perpetuate the myth of the Phoenix throughout the Middle Ages, and, later still, was treated as particularly authoritative during the Renaissance, when the bird became popular as a symbol of resurgent power, in men and institutions. The English poet Dryden caught the last echoes of the ancient belief in the myth of the Phoenix, with these lines:

So when the new-born
Phoenix first is seen
Her feathered subjects all
adore their queen,
And while she makes her
progress through the East,
From every grove her
numerous train's increased.

(Greek *phoinix*, 'Phoenician', purple.) A fabulous Arabian bird, adopted as a sign over chemists' shops because of its association with alchemy.

END NOTE

Harry Potter encountered the Sphinx, a Centaur, Dwarves, Giants, Mermaids, a Dragon, a Unicorn, a Phoenix and a Cockatrice (who took the form of a Basilisk) and a Hipogriff that may well have been a flying Griffin. A flying horse, similar to Pegasus, has an important role in *The Magician's Nephew*, one of the Narnia stories. Centaurs and a Unicorn also make appearances. Elves and Gnomes are important characters in the *Lord of the Rings* and Trolls and a Dragon can be found in *The Hobbit*.

Milton, on the other hand, conjures *Complicated monsters, head and tail, Scorpion and asp, and Amphisbaena dire, Cerastes horned, Hydrus, and Ellops drear* in *Paradise Lost*.

The world, it seems is full of beasts of myth and mystery.

Phœnix